NATIONAL BASEBALL
HALL OF FAME
AND MUSEUM®

MAP&GUIDE

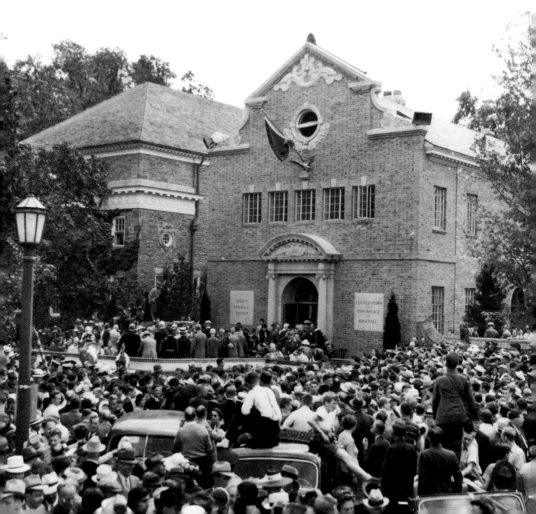

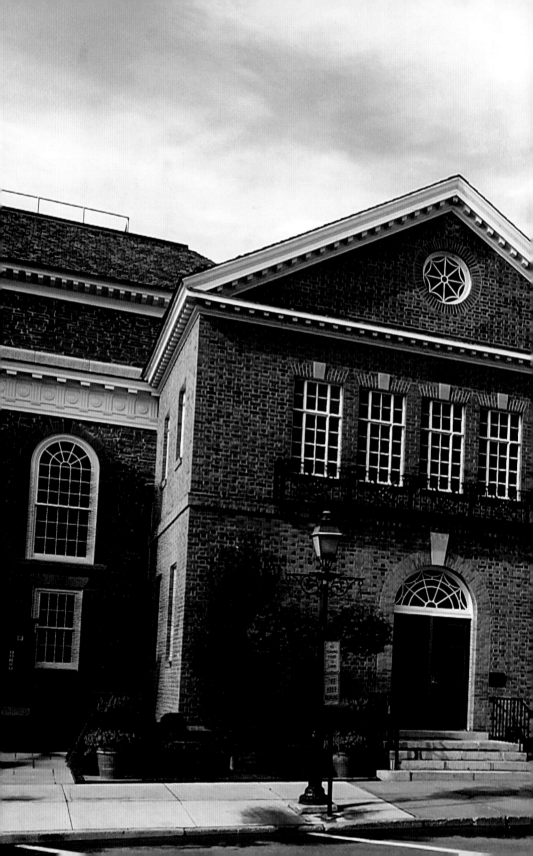

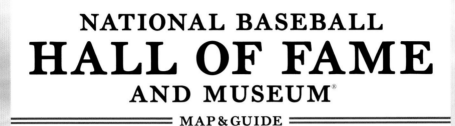

NATIONAL BASEBALL
HALL OF FAME
AND MUSEUM®

MAP & GUIDE

NATIONAL
★ ★ ★
BASEBALL

HALL OF FAME®

© Scala Publishers Ltd, 2006
Text © The National Baseball Hall of Fame and Museum
Pictures © The National Baseball Hall of Fame Library, Cooperstown, New York

First published in 2006 by
Scala Publishers Ltd
Northburgh House
10 Northburgh Street
London ECIV OAT
UK

ISBN 1 85759 427 4

Design and Project Management: Benjamin Shaykin
Copy Editor: Eleanor Hampton
Printed in China

10 9 8 7 6 5 4 3 2 1

Page 1: Opening day at the National Baseball Hall of Fame and Museum, June 12, 1939
This page: Uniform worn by Babe Ruth

Contents

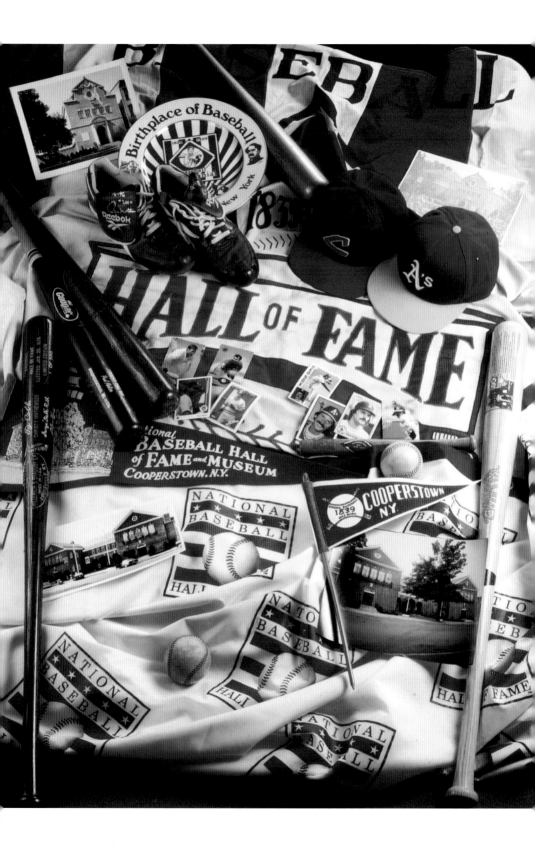

Foreword

If you stand in the middle of Main Street in Cooperstown, you might imagine that you have stepped back into the 1950s, into a Norman Rockwell painting.

For many years, the National Baseball Hall of Fame and Museum's exhibits and programs were a part of that brushstroke, but no longer. Today, Cooperstown still offers a generous slice of Americana, and the Museum artifacts continue to represent a step back in time to one's childhood. However, they are now presented as a state-of-the-art experience, and the Hall's outreach extends beyond the village, through the Catskill and Adirondack mountain regions to every corner of the United States.

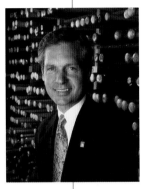

In 2005, the Hall of Fame completed a three-year, $20 million renovation project to improve the Museum experience. As you walk through the newly redesigned Baseball Hall of Fame and Museum, you'll notice fourteen new or improved exhibit and program spaces, plus 10,000 additional square feet of exhibition space. The Museum is now completely accessible for our visitors with special needs. In addition, exhibits have improved interactive technology and hands-on activities, and the collections are housed in a better and more consistent environment. Even the flow of the exhibit space has been changed, so that visitors experience a seamless tour from gallery to gallery.

This is the most sweeping renovation project in our history. We've always had the world's greatest baseball collection, and now we can share even more of it with our visitors. The renovation marks the Museum's seventh building redesign since opening its doors on June 12, 1939. Previous projects in 1950, 1958, 1968, 1980, 1989, and 1994 added exhibit space, the Hall of Fame Gallery, the Library, the Museum Store and Bookstore, and connected them all. The current project transformed the seven existing buildings into a single Museum facility.

When you walk through the Museum, allow your baseball memories to take control of the experience. You'll see baseball moments you've heard about for years, and you'll remember games you might have forgotten. We hope the memories come flooding back to you.

Whether you are planning your first visit to Cooperstown or have lost count of the number of visits you have made to the hallowed Hall, welcome. Enjoy your trip down memory lane.

My best wishes,

Dale Petroskey
President
National Baseball Hall
of Fame and Museum

Why Cooperstown?

The Origins of the National Baseball Hall of Fame and Museum

From humble beginnings, the National Baseball Hall of Fame and Museum has become one of the nation's most recognizable and popular educational institutions. The Museum is located in the pastoral village of Cooperstown in central New York State, nestled between the Catskill and Adirondack mountains, 70 miles west of Albany, the state capital.

The Baseball Hall of Fame officially opened its doors on June 12, 1939. Cooperstown represents a step back in time, with buildings dating to the early nineteenth century and red geraniums hanging from classically styled streetlights. More than 350,000 people travel to the village each year to pay tribute to our national pastime by visiting the Hall of Fame, an institution that honors excellence, preserves history, and connects generations.

The most popular question asked by baseball enthusiasts making their pilgrimage to the spiritual home of the game is, "Why Cooperstown?" The answer involves a commission, a tattered baseball, a philanthropist, and a centennial celebration.

The Mills Commission

The Mills Commission was appointed in 1905 to determine the origin of baseball. Albert G. Spalding, one of the game's pioneers, urged the formation of the committee following an article by Henry Chadwick, a famous early baseball writer, who contended that the sport evolved from the English game of rounders.

Seven prominent men comprised the commission. They were Col. A. G. Mills of New York, who played baseball before and during the Civil War and was the fourth president of the National League (1882–1884); Morgan G. Bulkeley, former governor and then U.S. senator of Connecticut, who served as the National League's first president in 1876; Arthur P. Gorman, U.S. senator from Maryland, a former player and former president of the National Baseball Club of Washington; Nicholas E. Young of Washington, D.C., a longtime player who was the first secretary and later the fifth president of the National League (1884–1902); Alfred J. Reach of Philadelphia and George Wright of Boston, both well-known businessmen and two of the most famous players of their day; and the president of the Amateur Athletic Union, James E. Sullivan of New York.

During its three-year study, the committee was deluged with communications on the subject. In support of Abner Doubleday's claim to have invented the game, the testimony of Abner Graves, a mining engineer from Denver, figured prominently in the committee's inquiry.

Graves and Doubleday had attended school together in Cooperstown. Doubleday was later appointed to the U.S. Military Academy at West Point, graduating in 1842. Subsequently he served in the

Artifacts and images from the opening of the National Baseball Hall of Fame and Museum, June 12, 1939.

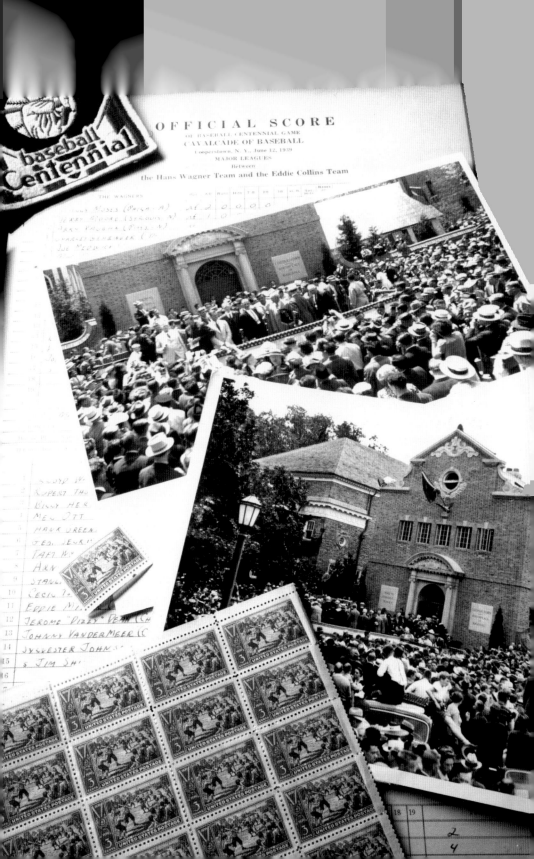

U.S.-Mexican War and the Civil War. According to historical records, he fired the first shot for the Union at Fort Sumter, South Carolina.

In his testimony, Graves claimed to have been present when Doubleday made changes to a local version of "town ball." As Graves described the game, one player tossed the ball straight in the air, allowing another player to hit the ball with a 4-inch-wide flat bat. Some twenty to fifty players, scattered about the field,

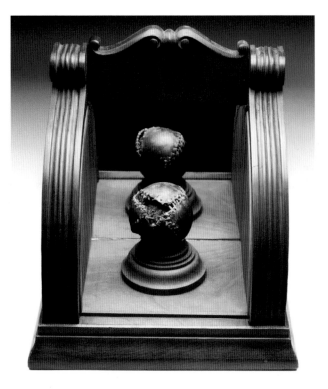

attempted to catch the ball before the batter could run to a goal 50 feet away. According to Graves, Doubleday used a stick to mark out a diamond-shaped field in the dirt. His other refinements to the rudimentary game included limiting the number of players and adding four bases (hence, the name *baseball*).

The committee's final report, on December 30, 1907, stated, in part, that "the first scheme for playing baseball, according to the best evidence obtainable to date, was devised by Abner Doubleday at Cooperstown, N.Y. in 1839."

The Baseball

The discovery of an old baseball in a dust-covered attic trunk in 1934 supported the committee's findings. The ball was located in a farmhouse in Fly Creek, a village 3 miles from Cooperstown, where the baseball—undersized, misshapen, and obviously homemade—was discovered. The stitched cover had been torn open, revealing stuffing of cloth instead of wool and cotton yarns, which comprise the interior of the modern baseball. The ball soon became known as the Doubleday Baseball.

The Philanthropist

Soon after its discovery, the baseball was purchased for $5 by Stephen C. Clark, a Cooperstown resident and philanthropist. Clark conceived the idea of displaying the ball, along with such other baseball objects as could be obtained, in a room in the Village Club, which now houses the Cooperstown village offices. The small

---

ABOVE: The Doubleday Baseball, from the mythical first game in 1839, found in an attic near Cooperstown in 1934. OPPOSITE: Abner Graves's letters to the Mills Commission.

one-room exhibition attracted tremendous public interest. With the assistance of Alexander Cleland, who had been associated with Clark in other endeavors, support was sought for the establishment of a national baseball museum.

Ford Frick, then president of the National League, was especially enthusiastic. He obtained the backing of Kenesaw Mountain Landis, baseball's first commissioner, and William Harridge, president of the American League. Contributions and historically significant baseball memorabilia soon poured in from all parts of the country as word spread.

Baseball's Centennial

Coincidentally, in 1935, plans were also being formulated for an appropriate celebration in Cooperstown to mark baseball's upcoming 100th anniversary, which would take place in 1939. Frick proposed that a hall of fame be established as part of the shrine to honor the game's immortals.

Members of the Baseball Writers' Association of America were enlisted to select the greats who were to be honored. The first election was conducted in January 1936, and five players were selected—Ty Cobb, Babe Ruth, Honus Wagner, Christy Mathewson, and Walter Johnson.

The National Baseball Hall of Fame and Museum was officially dedicated on June 12, 1939. The game's four ranking executives of the period—Landis, Frick, Harridge, and William G. Bramham, president of the National Association of Professional Baseball Leagues—participated in the ribbon cutting. Of the twenty-five men who had been elected to the Hall of Fame to that point, eleven were still living, and each journeyed to Cooperstown to attend the centennial celebration. As part of the festivities, a baseball postage stamp commemorating the occasion was placed on sale that day at the Cooperstown Post Office, with Postmaster General James A. Farley presiding.

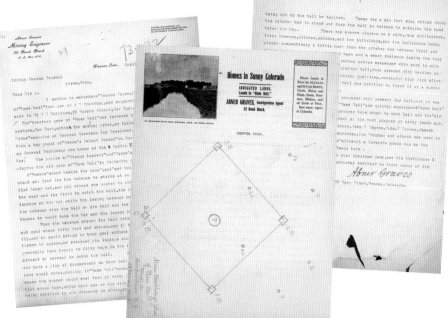

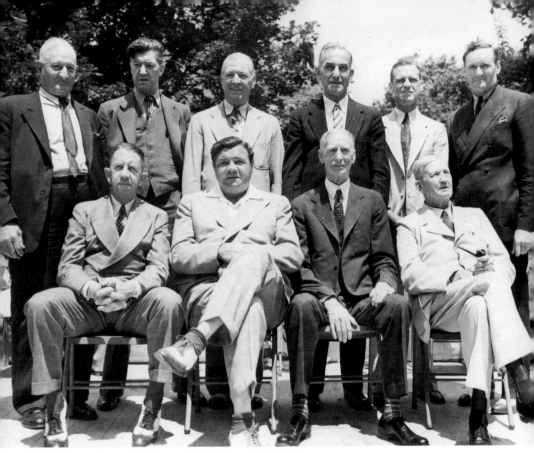

ABOVE: The first four classes of living inductees gathered for the opening of the Hall of Fame, June 12, 1939. Back row, left to right: Honus Wagner, Grover Cleveland Alexander, Tris Speaker, Nap Lajoie, George Sisler, and Walter Johnson. Front row, left to right: Eddie Collins, Babe Ruth, Connie Mack, and Cy Young. The eleventh living inductee, Ty Cobb, missed the photo due to travel delays. OPPOSITE: A pennant from the 1922 Yankees.

New Research

After the commission reported its findings in 1908, many of the game's historians disputed Graves's account, noting that many of the innovations he attributed to Doubleday were already being practiced in the 1830s. The original Mills Commission papers, long thought to have been burned but finally discovered in 1999, support the view of many researchers that baseball developed from and along with other bat-and-ball games earlier in the nineteenth century. One day, historians may determine that Abner Graves's testimony, which covered a period when the widely played game of town ball was undergoing rapid changes, captures the point in time when changes to the game arrived in one typical American community and caused a minor revolution on the sandlot.

Nevertheless, such a finding will not diminish the Mills Commission's contribution to our national pastime a century ago. By collecting the memories of many early fans and players while they were still living, the committee created a treasure trove of early baseball history that would otherwise have been lost. Moreover, by identifying Cooperstown as the site of the sport's origin, the Mills Commission initiated the process that ultimately established a home for the sport—The National Baseball Hall of Fame and Museum.

Evolution of the Museum and Library

Since 1939, several significant enhancements have taken place at the Museum. Expansions in 1950 and 1980 added much more exhibit space, while the Hall of Fame Gallery was dedicated in 1958. In 1994, the original Library, which had opened in 1968, was renovated and connected to the Museum. In 2005, the Museum completed a three-year, $20 million renovation project to create a safer environment for visitors, provide smoother traffic flow through the Museum's galleries, better manage and control the climate for artifacts, and provide a greater presence of interactive technology for visitors.

Representing all aspects of baseball—both on the field and in our culture—the Museum collections total 36,000 three-dimensional artifacts (including bats, balls, gloves, caps, helmets, uniforms, shoes, trophies, and awards) and

132,000 baseball cards. All artifacts in the Museum's collections have been donated.

Founded in 1939 as part of The National Baseball Hall of Fame and Museum, the National Baseball Library is by far the largest repository of baseball information in the world. The Library is responsible for the acquisition, organization, preservation, and dissemination of all archival material related to the history of baseball and its impact on culture and society.

The National Baseball Library contains 2.6 million items that are housed in climate-controlled areas and maintained by a professional staff using state-of-the-art archival techniques. The photo collection contains more than 500,000 historic images of players, teams, ballparks, and other baseball subjects. In addition, the Library's film, video, and recorded sound archives contain more than 10,000 hours of footage and audio recordings dating back to the late nineteenth century, including an extensive collection of Hollywood movies featuring baseball.

The Library is a public facility where numerous researchers and Museum visitors are served annually. While most patrons are independent baseball fans conducting research, others using the facilities have included such esteemed authors as George Plimpton, Roger Kahn, and George Will; officials from many major and minor league clubs; former big league players; writers

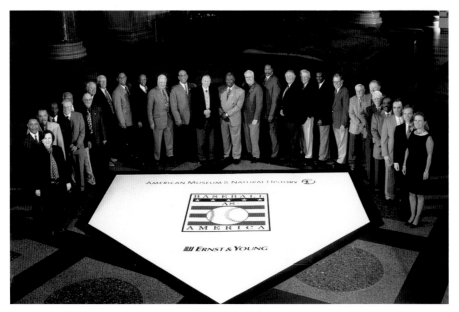

ABOVE: In 2002, twenty-four members of the Hall of Fame gathered at the American Museum of Natural History in New York City for the grand opening of Baseball As America. OPPOSITE TOP: Jane Forbes Clark, chairman, National Baseball Hall of Fame and Museum. OPPOSITE BELOW: The Boston Red Sox and Detroit Tigers played at Doubleday Field in the 2005 Hall of Fame Game.

from the *New York Times*, *USA Today*, and the *Wall Street Journal*; researchers from television shows such as *Jeopardy!*; and students of all ages. Whether it's simply answering a question or fielding a request from the White House for information for a presidential speech, the research department answers approximately 60,000 research inquiries annually.

The National Baseball Hall of Fame Today

In August 2000, the board of directors of the Museum elected the founder's granddaughter, Jane Forbes Clark, to be chair. In 1999, Dale Petroskey became the Museum's fifth president. Under their leadership, the Museum has continued to broaden its educational outreach and has created an endowment to ensure its long-term financial security. In 2002, Baseball As America, an exhibition of 500 Museum

artifacts, opened a four-year national tour to much acclaim at the American Museum of Natural History in New York City. The exhibit will have visited ten world-class museums across the country before the end of 2006. The tour was recently extended to include four more cities in 2007 and 2008. The national tour of Baseball As America is sponsored by Ernst & Young. Published by National Geographic, *Baseball As America: Seeing Ourselves Through Our National Game* is the official companion volume to the tour.

The Hall of Fame's education programs extend the Museum's reach to children throughout the United States. America Grows Inning by Inning—an extensive series of thematic lessons—teaches core curriculum subjects using the game of baseball as a hands-on foundation for helping students learn. In addition to on-site school visits, the Museum delivers interactive programs to classrooms outside of Cooperstown via distance learning. Through partnerships with Ball State University in Muncie, Indiana, and Project View in Schenectady, New York, one-hour to half-day electronic field trips and videoconferences have been enjoyed by nearly 100 million students nationwide in the last five years. Additionally, the Museum's education outreach features 500 videoconferences each year.

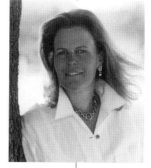

As a part of its public programming for visitors of all ages, the Museum also offers an extensive year-round calendar of entertaining and informative events designed for families and baseball scholars alike. From roundtable discussions with Hall of Fame members to Sandlot Stories, featuring staff and visiting experts highlighting baseball's rich history, to gallery talks, treasure hunts, concerts, movies, and plays, the Baseball Hall of Fame presents more than 1,000 educational events each year.

Additionally, Hall of Fame Weekend, featuring the Induction Ceremony and dozens of returning Hall of Fame members, highlights the year's schedule of events. The annual Hall of Fame Game, a tradition since the Museum's inception in 1939, features two major league teams in an exhibition contest at legendary Doubleday Field, and draws thousands for an afternoon game at the home of baseball. And after its inaugural effort in 2005, the Hall of Fame now offers a Hall of Fame Fantasy Camp each October featuring Hall of Fame members.

The Baseball Hall of Fame has become an international destination that chronicles the evolution of America's national pastime. From humble beginnings and a small collection of artifacts in the mid-1930s, the Hall of Fame has evolved into a cultural showcase, where people come to learn about the past and soon discover that baseball is the common thread of our national spirit.

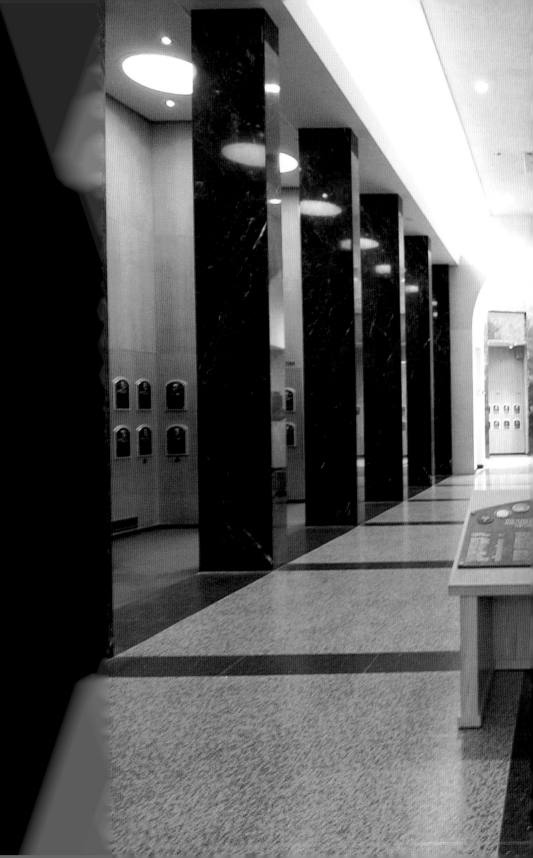

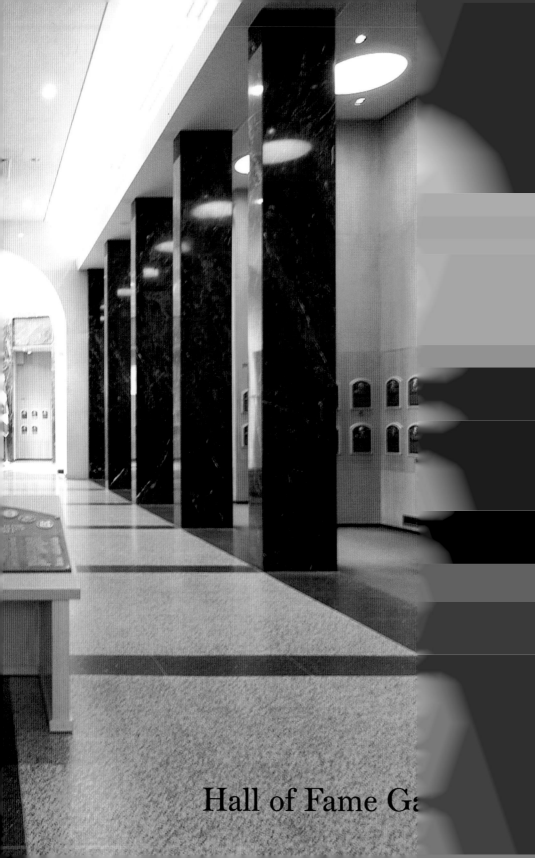

Hall of Fame Ga

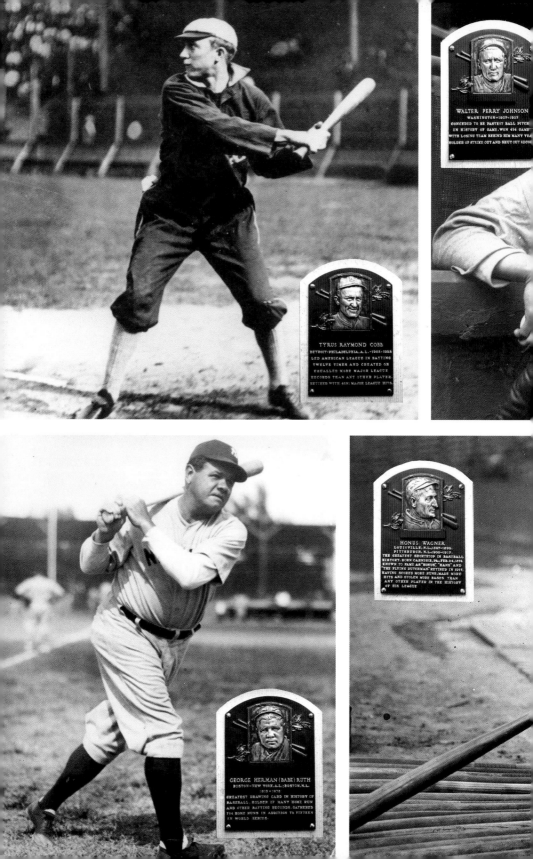

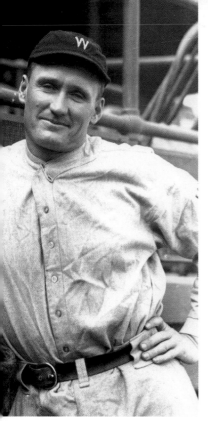

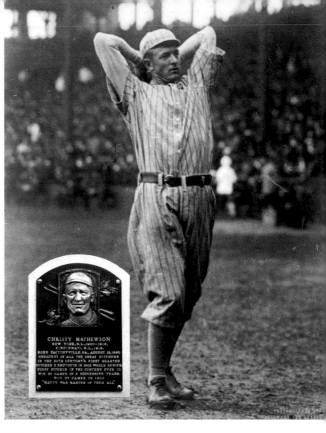

CHRISTY MATHEWSON
NEW YORK, N.L. 1900-1916.
CINCINNATI, N.L. 1916.
BORN FACTORYVILLE, PA., AUGUST 12, 1880
GREATEST OF ALL THE GREAT PITCHERS
IN THE 20TH CENTURY'S FIRST QUARTER
PITCHED 3 SHUTOUTS IN 1905 WORLD SERIES
FIRST PITCHER OF THE CENTURY EVER TO
WIN 30 GAMES IN 3 SUCCESSIVE YEARS.
WON 37 GAMES IN 1908
"MATTY WAS MASTER OF THEM ALL"

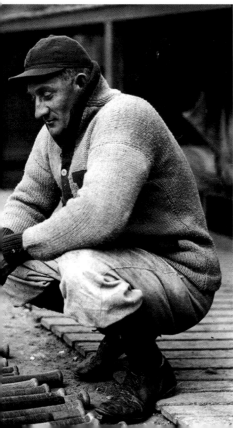

The First Five

Stroll through the Hall of Fame Gallery and stand among the game's greatest contributors. Each bronze plaque honors the player, umpire, executive, or manager for his contributions to the game, from the first five electees in 1936—Babe Ruth, Walter Johnson, Christy Mathewson, Ty Cobb, and Honus Wagner—to the current class of inductees.

The most hallowed ground in all of baseball, the Hall of Fame Gallery symbolizes the monumental odds of earning a plaque in Cooperstown. Just one player in every 100 talented enough to play in the major leagues earns a spot in the Hall of Fame.

The first class of plaques is displayed in the rotunda of the Gallery, with others placed by year of induction beginning on the right side of the marble and oak room. Current and recent inductees are also celebrated in the rotunda at the head of the Gallery.

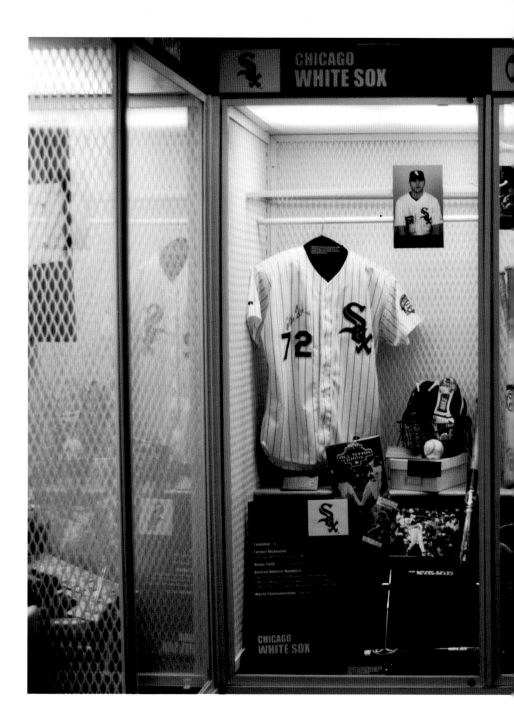

Lockers feature artifacts from the last ten years for every major league team in Today's Game.

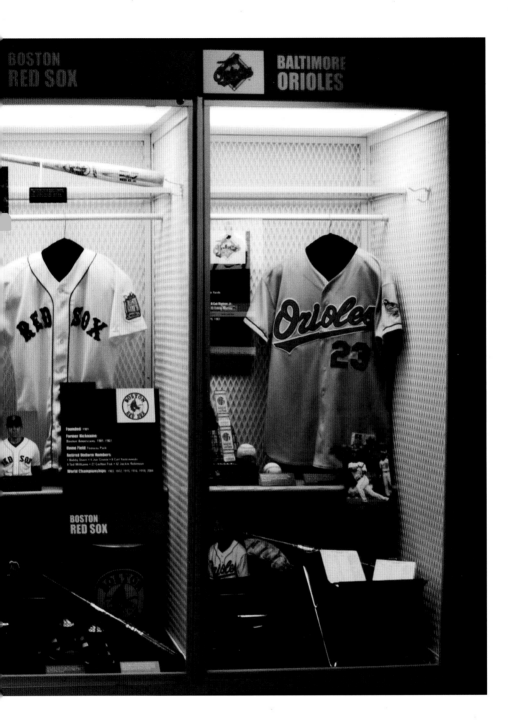

Second Floor

Cooperstown Room

Learn about the Museum's origins, the history of the National Baseball Hall of Fame and Museum, and Cooperstown's special role in the national pastime.

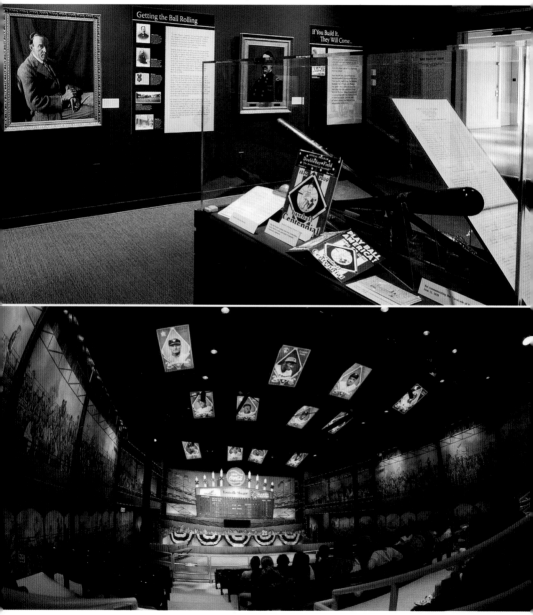

Grandstand Theater

Prepare for an emotional journey through baseball history with *The Baseball Experience*, an entertaining thirteen-minute all-digital multimedia presentation in the Museum's main theater.

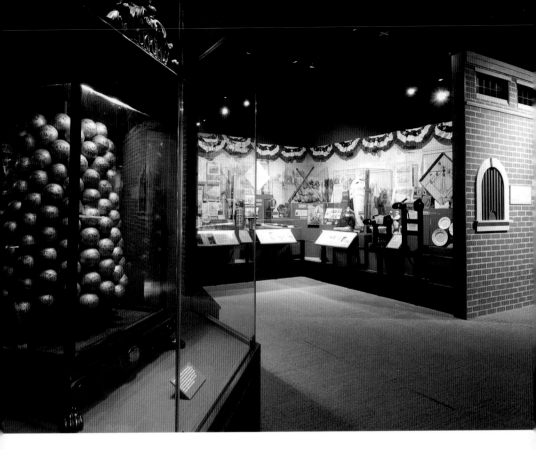

Taking the Field
The 19th Century

Taking the Field: The 19th Century offers a comprehensive examination of baseball's origins and early professional clubs, featuring more than 150 artifacts and graphics.

The exhibit spotlights several hands-on activities. Visitors can leaf through a scrapbook of a century of worldwide baseball. A stereoscope depicts authentic baseball scenes from the nineteenth century. Visitors can also use a telegraph key to tap out baseball plays in Morse code, just as newspaper reporters did in the second half of the century.

Ambient nineteenth-century baseball music complements the exhibit, while a video presentation of baseball plays, re-created by period performers, illustrates nineteenth-century baseball rules. Custom-made Victorian wallpaper, produced by the American Paper-Staining Manufactory at the Farmers' Museum in Cooperstown, adorns the exhibit walls.

ABOVE: The entrance to Taking the Field: The 19th Century greets visitors with the Eckford Ball Case, featuring souvenirs from the Eckford club team of the late 1800s.

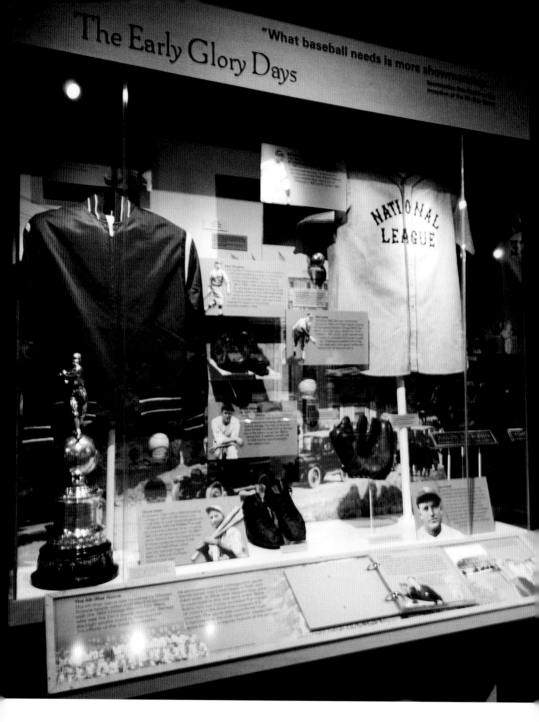

Baseball's Timeline

Learn about the game's greatest teams, players, moments, and stories through original artifacts, compelling photographs, and classic ephemera, with a chronological presentation of baseball history.

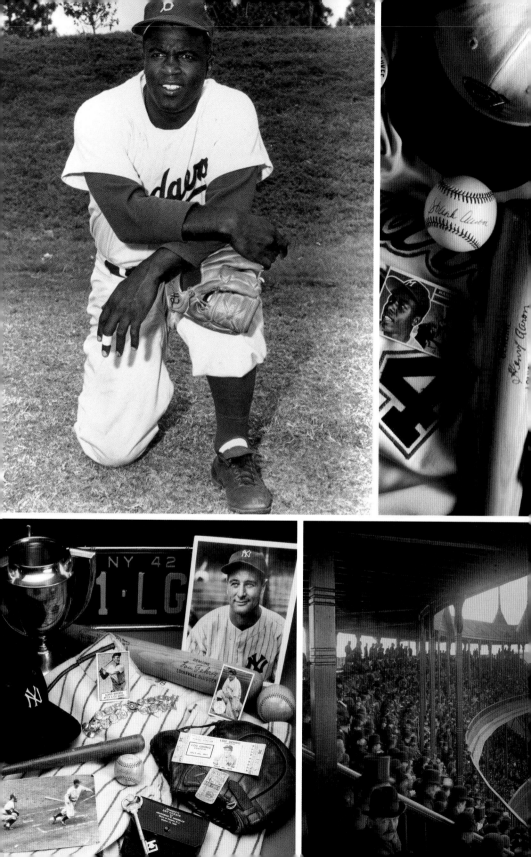

Babe Ruth Gallery

Baseball's first superstar, Babe Ruth, revolutionized the sport with his monster swing and larger-than-life personality. In this gallery, learn about George Herman "Babe" Ruth, the player and the man.

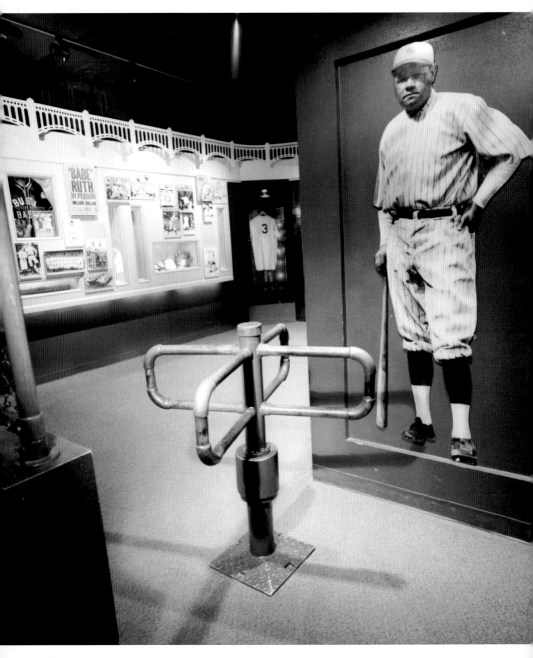

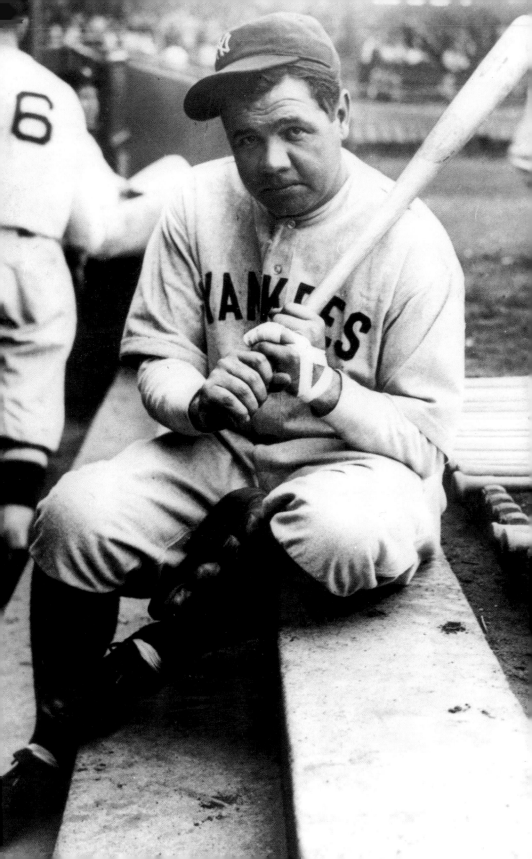

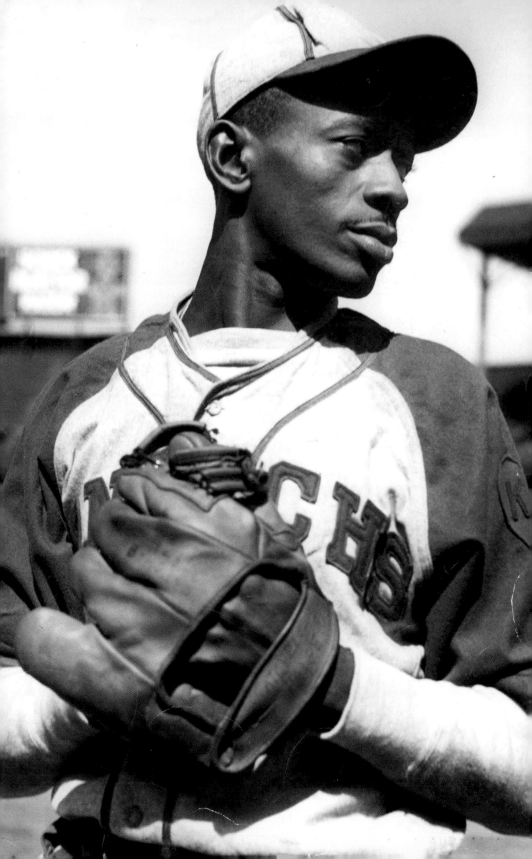

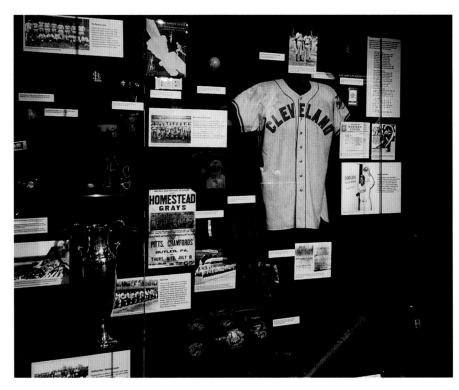

Pride and Passion
The African American Baseball Experience

Dedicated to the men and women whose passion for our national game helped them triumph over obstacles brought about by prejudice and intolerance in our nation, this exhibit recognizes the contributions of African Americans in baseball.

The exhibit pays tribute to 100 years of black baseball, from Civil War days through integration, with special recognition of the legacy of Hall of Famer Jackie Robinson, whose actions on and off the field served as the catalyst for progress, both in our game and in our society.

The exhibit features lessons on creating opportunity, barnstorming teams and players, separate leagues, the evolution of the famed Negro leagues, changing opportunities when African Americans joined the major league ranks, and the post-integration era of African Americans in executive and managerial roles in the game.

Artifacts include awards, documents, uniforms and equipment from stars such as Robinson, Satchel Paige, Buck Leonard, and Frank Robinson.

OPPOSITE: Kansas City Monarchs star pitcher Satchel Paige, a member of the Baseball Hall of Fame. ABOVE: An exhibit honoring African American contributions to baseball was rededicated in April 2006.

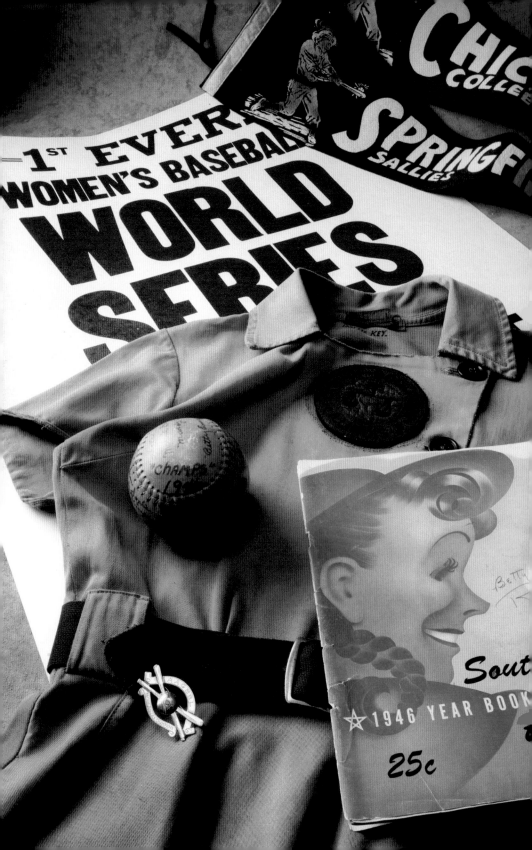

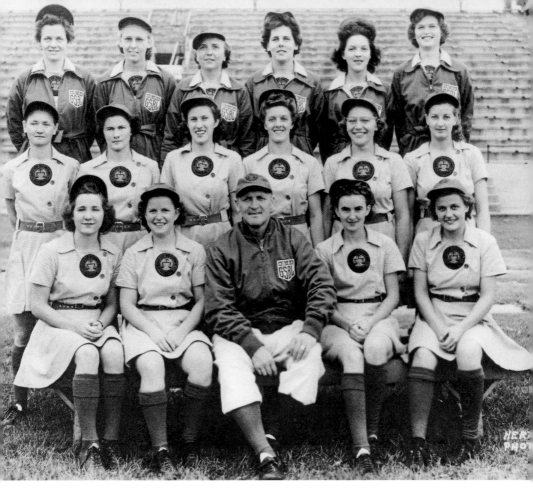

Diamond Dreams
Women in Baseball

The contributions of women pioneers to the game are celebrated and revered in one of the Museum's most popular exhibits. Featuring the memories and stars of the All-American Girls Professional Baseball League (AAGPBL), and highlighted by the feats of other women on and off the field, the Museum's Diamond Dreams exhibit details the significant impact women have had on the game.

The original exhibit helped establish the story line for the 1992 theatrical release *A League of Their Own*, and many of the stories from the real-life league, as well as the movie, are on display. Learn about pioneers such as Alta Weiss, Ila Borders, and other women who have left their mark on our national pastime.

OPPOSITE: Artifacts from the All-American Girls Professional Baseball League. ABOVE: The 1943 Rockford Peaches, along with other teams from the AAGPBL, are featured in Diamond Dreams.

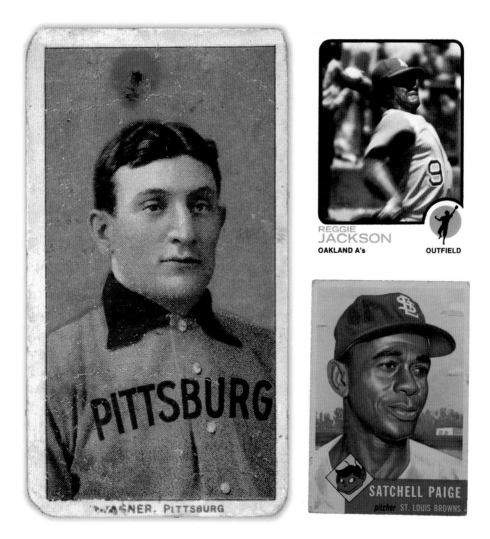

WAGNER, PITTSBURG

REGGIE
JACKSON
OAKLAND A's   OUTFIELD

SATCHELL PAIGE
pitcher ST. LOUIS BROWNS

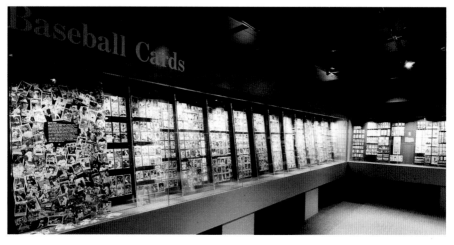

Baseball Cards

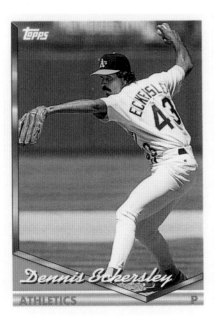

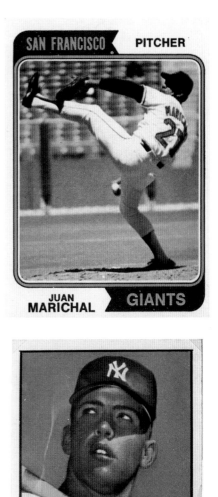

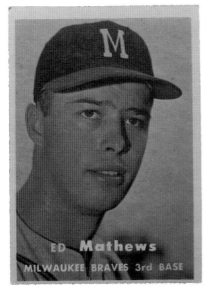

Baseball Cards

A selection from the more than 132,000 baseball cards in the Museum's collection is on display, featuring cards from every era. The 1909 T206 Honus Wagner tobacco card (OPPOSITE, TOP LEFT) highlights the display case, and is a favorite with fans.

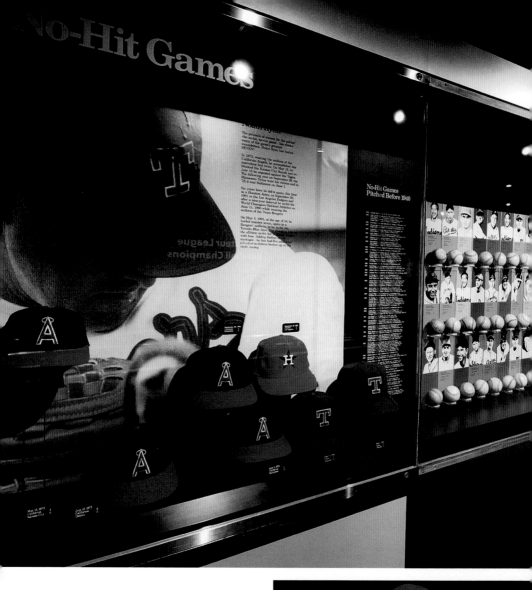

No-Hit Games

See a baseball from every no-hitter thrown
since the Museum's opening in 1939,
along with caps from each of Nolan Ryan's
record-setting seven no-hitters.

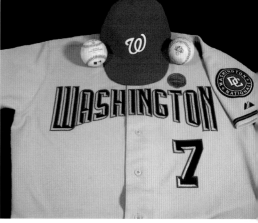

Today's Game

Today's Game combines the Museum's most recent artifact acquisitions with video highlights to re-create the look and feel of a major league clubhouse.

Today's Game features more than 250 artifacts from the last ten baseball seasons, with "lockers" for all thirty major league teams. Among the recent artifacts are the bat used by Andruw Jones to record his fiftieth home run of the 2005 season, which was also the 300th home run of his career; the spikes worn by Greg Maddux when he notched his 300th career victory; and the batting helmet worn by Jimmy Rollins in the 2005 season finale when he hit safely in his thirty-sixth straight game.

OPPOSITE BELOW: Washington Nationals artifacts from their inaugural season in 2005. BELOW: Each major league team is represented with artifacts from the last ten seasons in the Today's Game exhibit.

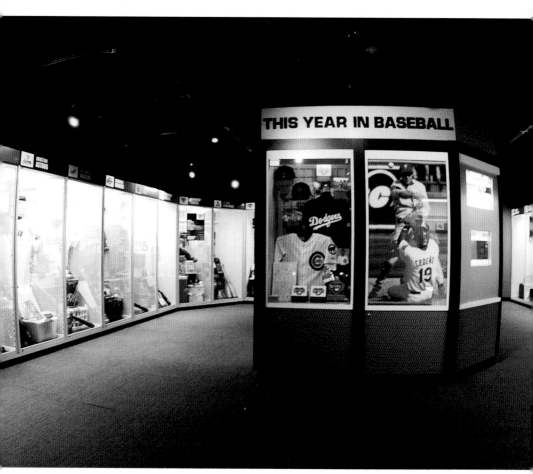

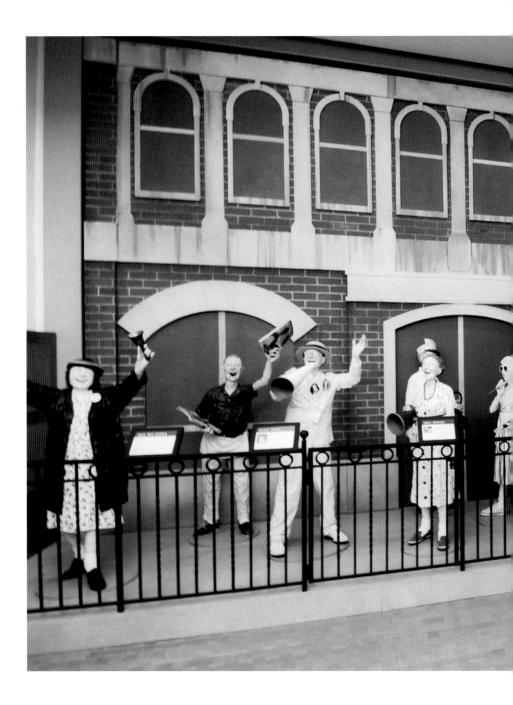

Fabric mâché statues of favorite fans at ballparks across the country greet visitors at the third-floor entrance to Sacred Ground.

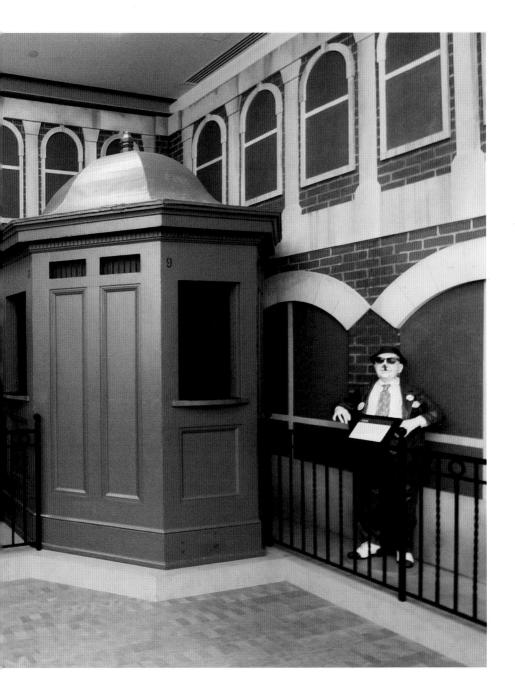

Third Floor

Sacred Ground

Sacred Ground explores the ballparks of our great game's past and present, with more than 200 artifacts documenting the fan experience at baseball's hallowed fields of green.

Among the most notable artifacts in the exhibit are a scoreboard pinwheel from Comiskey Park, a ticket booth

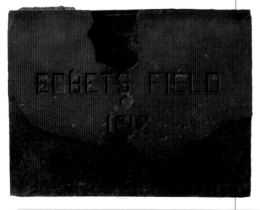

from Yankee Stadium, a turnstile from the Polo Grounds, the cornerstone from Ebbets Field, Walter Johnson's locker from Griffith Stadium, and the Pirates' on-deck circle from Forbes Field.

The exhibit also includes a special interactive section dedicated to music at the ballpark. Visitors can hear the distinctive sounds from various ballparks and learn the history of the classic baseball song "Take Me Out to the Ball Game."

Ballparks of the past come to life in a computer interactive, where visitors can "walk" through Boston's South End Grounds Grand Pavilion (in existence from 1888 to 1894) by viewing an enormous 14-by-8-foot curved screen and seeing what the ballpark looked like in its heyday.

ABOVE: The cornerstone from Ebbets Field. OPPOSITE TOP: A famed scoreboard pinwheel from Comiskey Park. OPPOSITE BOTTOM: Sacred Ground retells the fan experience.

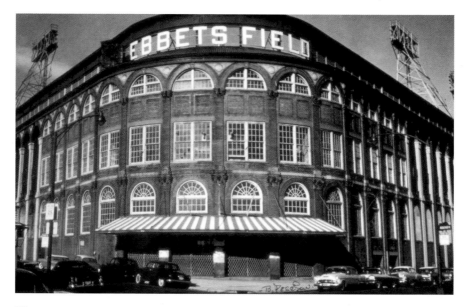

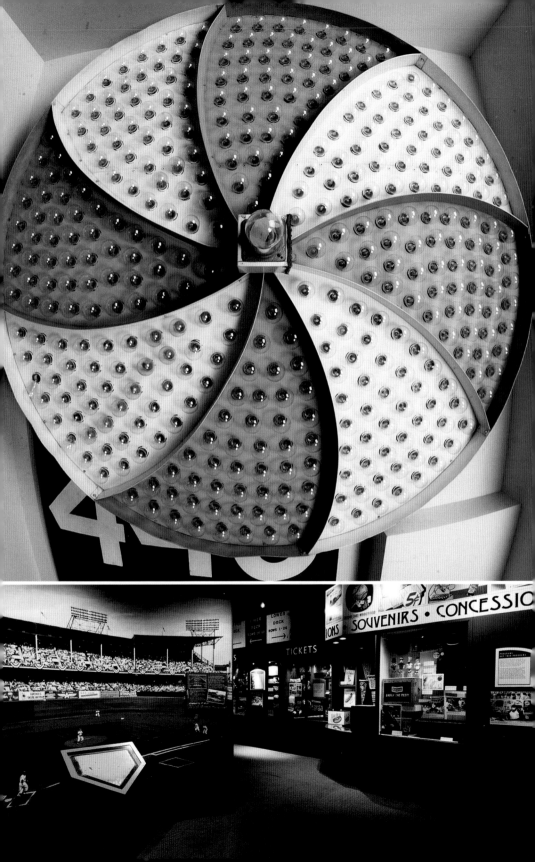

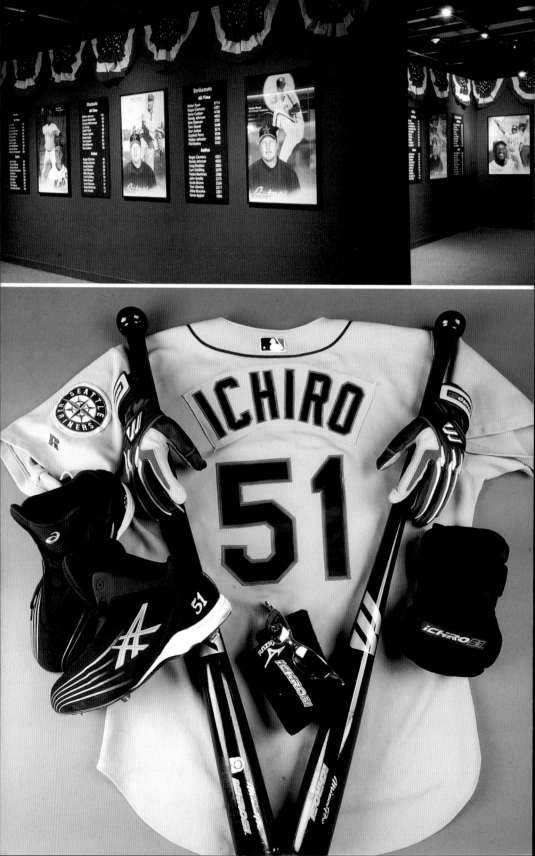

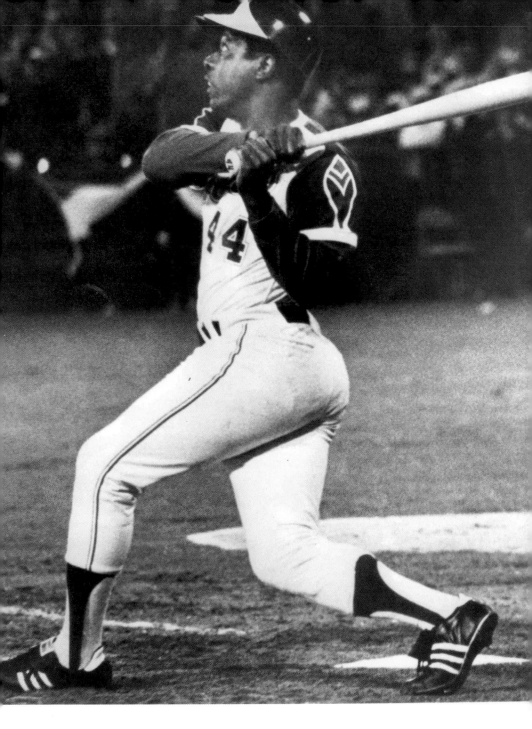

Records Room

View the statistical leaders by category, both all-time and active players, while admiring some of baseball's most prestigious hardware such as the Cy Young, Gold Glove, Silver Slugger, and Most Valuable Player awards, as well as special exhibits dedicated to record performances.

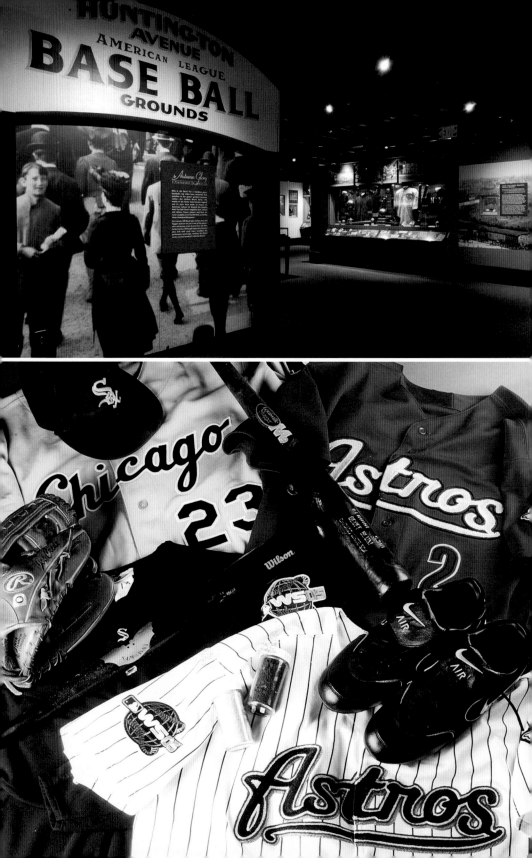

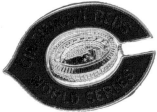

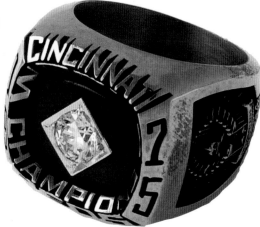

Autumn Glory
A Postseason Celebration

Autumn Glory: A Postseason Celebration commemorates more than 100 years of postseason and World Series memories. Featuring artifacts, documents, photographs, and interactive displays, the 2,400-square-foot exhibit highlights numerous classic postseason moments and baseball's October heroes. From the last-out ball of the first modern World Series in 1903 to items from the most recent World Series, every postseason is represented through artifacts and interactive stories.

The exhibit contains all 165 World Series programs and hundreds of postseason game-related items, including four World Championship trophies; the glove worn by Willie Mays in the 1954 World Series to make "The Catch"; World Series jewelry such as championship rings, charms, pendants, and press pins; and an exhibit dedicated to the most recent World Series champion.

Three interactive displays allow visitors to dig deeper into every World Series from the premodern era (1884–1900) through today. More than forty audio-video highlights of classic postseason moments can be seen or heard, and composite stats from every World Series team, including line scores, attendance figures, and extensive record books, can be viewed.

OPPOSITE: Autumn Glory features artifacts from the first modern World Series in 1903 through the most recent Fall Classic. ABOVE: The exhibit features every World Series ring and press pin, including the 1975 World Series ring presented to the Cincinnati Reds.

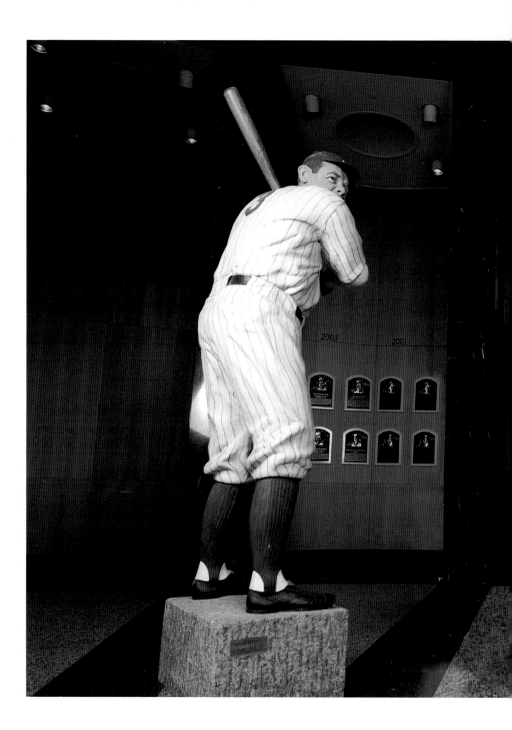

Life-size sculptures of Babe Ruth and Ted Williams were each carved from single pieces of basswood and donated to the Museum by artist Armand LaMontagne.

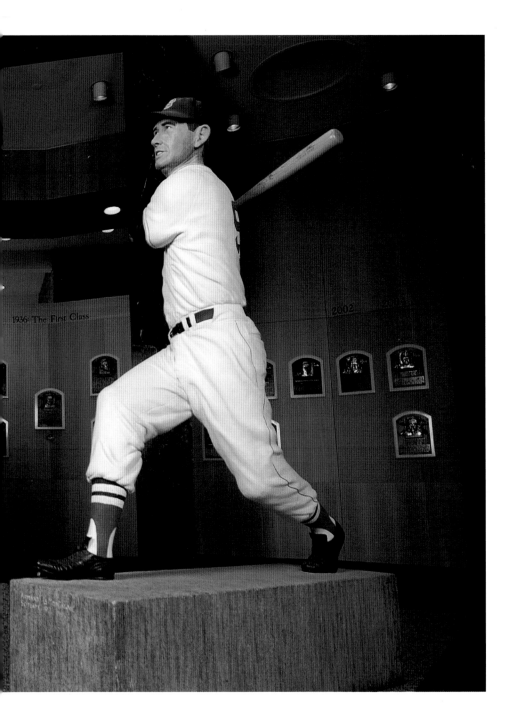

First Floor

Inductee Row

See artifacts from the current class of Hall of Fame inductees and relive Induction Day through photographs of all living Hall of Fame members before entering the hallowed Hall of Fame Gallery. BELOW: Ryne Sandberg and Wade Boggs share their Hall of Fame induction moment during 2005 Hall of Fame Weekend.

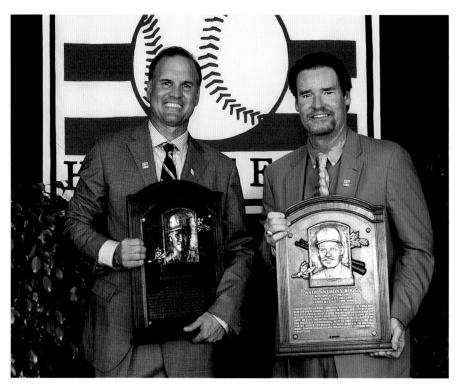

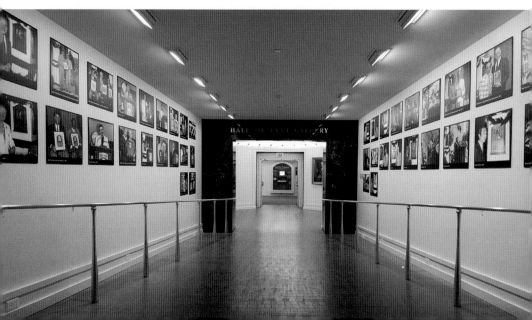

The Frank and Peggy Steele Art Gallery

Original works of art—paintings, sculptures, and renderings—commemorate America's love affair with baseball.

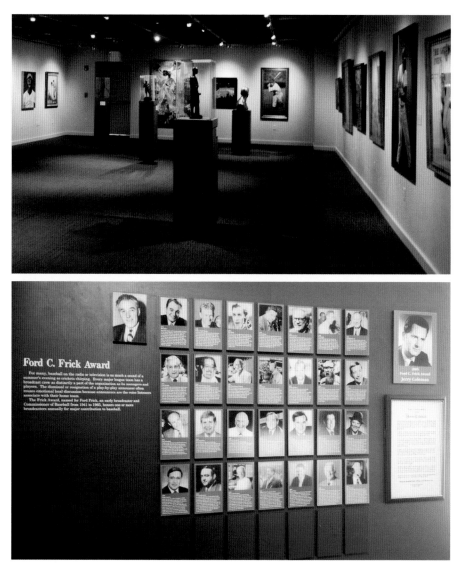

Scribes and Mikemen

Hear famed audio recordings of baseball's memorable moments while learning about the winners of the prestigious Ford C. Frick and J. G. Taylor Spink awards.

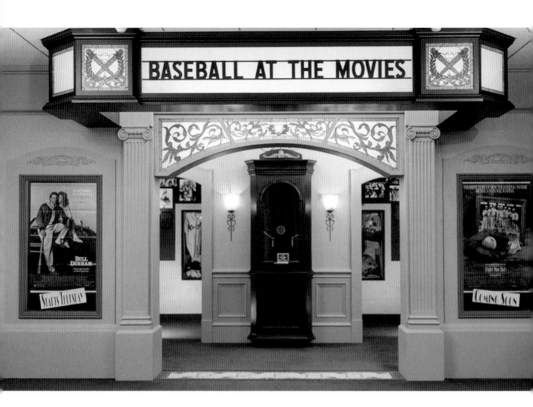

Baseball at the Movies

Explore the intimate relationship that baseball and Hollywood have shared through the years with artifacts from cinema blockbusters and pop culture favorites.

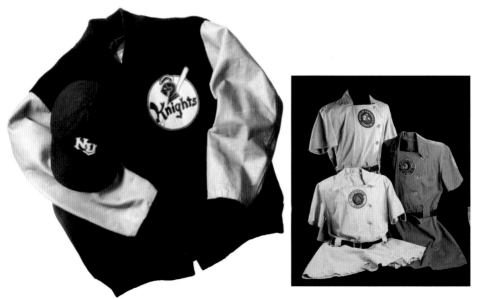

Sandlot Kids' Clubhouse

The Sandlot Kids' Clubhouse features more than fifteen youth-friendly experiences. The exhibit contains many interactive components, such as a magnetic game called Batter Up! that teaches baseball fielding positions and mathematical concepts. A vertical measurement chart represents the heights of several famous players from the major leagues, Negro leagues, and the All-American Girls Professional Baseball League.

In the discovery area, visitors can rummage through discovery drawers filled with Museum artifacts. A signature feature of the discovery area is an interactive literacy corner called What's On Next. There, a 37-inch flat-panel LCD screen features several programs, including a message from Hall of Famer Ozzie Smith; *Curious George Plays Baseball*, narrated by Hall of Fame member Brooks Robinson; and *Players in Pigtails*, narrated by AAGPBL veteran Terry Donahue. Additionally, *Garfield* creator Jim Davis has contributed a rendering of Garfield the cat dressed as a ballpark vendor.

The Sandlot Kids' Clubhouse is funded through the generosity of Ball State University of Muncie, Indiana; the Best Buy Children's Foundation of Richfield, Minnesota; and the Ruth and Vernon Taylor Foundation of Denver.

OPPOSITE: Artifacts featured in Baseball at the Movies include the jacket worn by Robert Redford in *The Natural* and tunics worn during the filming of *A League of Their Own*. BELOW: The Sandlot Kids' Clubhouse provides an educational experience for visitors ages 4–10.

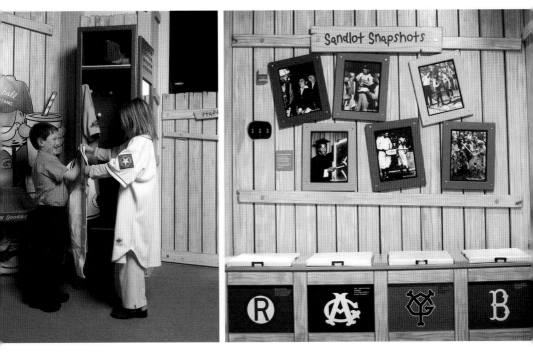

The National Baseball Hall of Fame Library

The National Baseball Hall of Fame Library was founded in 1939 as part of the National Baseball Hall of Fame and Museum. Its mission is to collect, organize, and preserve the complete history of our national pastime as recorded in all media formats for the use of baseball fans and researchers.

The collection at the Library has been acquired through the generosity of baseball fans, researchers, teams, and players. Donors are accorded special recognition and privileges. If you would like to help us document our national pastime and preserve its heritage for future generations, please consider becoming a donor.

The A. Bartlett Giamatti Research Center

The A. Bartlett Giamatti Research Center, rededicated in memory of the former commissioner of baseball on July 26, 1998, can help you find answers to your baseball questions, large or small. Our vast collection of baseball books, magazines, newspaper clippings, and archival material is a rich source of information on baseball and related topics.

Today, the Library contains the world's most extensive collec-

tion of archival material devoted exclusively to baseball. This is a public facility, and thousands of researchers, Museum visitors, callers, and correspondents are served annually.

The Library is open from 9 A.M. until 5 P.M. on weekdays. On-site appointments and off-site research assistance can be arranged by calling (607) 547-0330.

Recorded Media Department

The Library contains more than 12,000 hours of moving image and sound recordings. The collection includes interviews, game highlights, television and radio broadcasts, animation, and music. Selections from the collection are featured daily in the Library's Bullpen Theater.

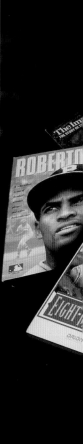

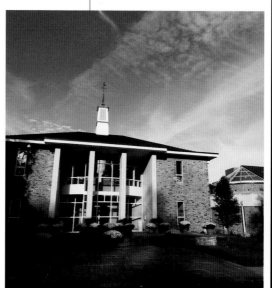

Many of the selections within the Library's Recorded Media Department are available for purchase from the Hall of Fame.

To contact the Recorded Media Department, please call (607) 547-0314.

Photograph Department

More than 500,000 images of players, teams, stadiums, events, and other subjects are housed in the Library. The collection includes black-and-white prints, color prints, slides, transparencies, and negatives.

Most of the photographs in our collection are available for reproduction. We will gladly send a limited selection of photocopies for your review. Please note that a research fee of $25 per hour may be charged for extensive requests. All photograph reproduction rates are per image and are subject to change. Orders may be paid by check, money order, or credit card.

To contact the Photograph Department, please call (607) 547-0372 or visit the extensive photo collection online at www.baseballhalloffame.org.

The Hall of Fame Library features more than 2.6 million documents, including more than 12,000 hours of recorded audio and video.

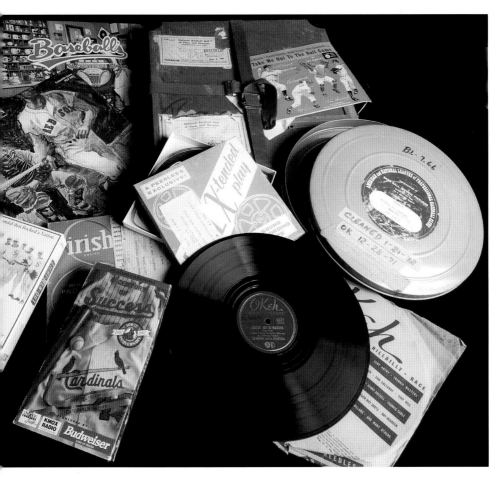

Unique Artifacts Reveal Baseball's Zany, Quirky Sides

If the wee people of County Tipperary, Ireland, could have only known their legacy would forever be preserved at the National Baseball Hall of Fame and Museum in Cooperstown, perhaps baseball would be considered alongside St. Patrick's Day, Claddagh rings, and the University of Notre Dame as distinctly Irish traditions that are revered around the world today.

Though we'll never know precisely how or to what degree the wee people participated in baseball's early incarnations, Cooperstown counts a petrified "mitt" from the pint-size residents of the central Ireland county among the oldest and most unique objects in the Museum's collections of more than 35,000 three-dimensional artifacts and 130,000 baseball cards.

While more than 6,400 baseballs, 2,000 tickets, 1,800 bats, 850 jerseys, 600 caps, and 450 gloves are the most numerous and recognizable artifacts in the Museum's historic collection, a number of unique—and often revealing—items are also housed in the 50,000-square-foot Museum.

If there are multiple ways to tell a story about a moment in baseball history or to describe the personalities of some of the game's most colorful participants, the collections in Cooperstown ensure that generations of baseball fans will be reminded about the quirky characters, zany promotions, and offbeat incidents in the enduring history of our national pastime.

Nearly seven decades after opening, the Museum maintains a proactive policy in collecting artifacts from milestones and record achievements, with many collections taking place soon after the events happen. Ongoing artifact acquisition leads to new revelations of baseball's

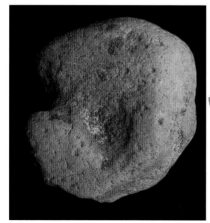

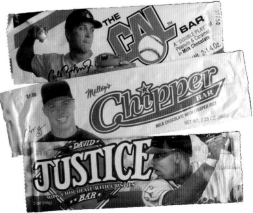

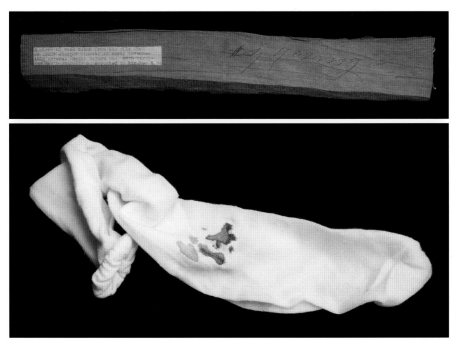

Unique artifacts in the Museum's collections include (OPPOSITE LEFT) a petrified mitt used by the wee people of County Tipperary, Ireland; (OPPOSITE RIGHT) candy bar wrappers from confections named after superstars Cal Ripken Jr., Chipper Jones, and David Justice; (TOP) a piece of wood, believed to be the last ever chopped by Cy Young; and (ABOVE) the blood-soaked sock worn by Curt Schilling in Game Two of the 2004 World Series.

past. An internal accessions committee meets monthly to review potential donations from fans, collectors, and those interested in having their baseball memories contributed to Cooperstown.

Only by the generosity of players, organizations, and fans has the story of baseball's past been so richly preserved. The role of preserving history can take many forms, even through the oddly eccentric. "To me, it shows how baseball permeates every facet of life," says Peter C. Clark, curator of collections for the Museum. "These far-out items are connected to baseball."

Clark, who has worked for the Hall of Fame since 1969, counts among the quirkiest artifacts in Cooperstown a razor blade used by Cy Young in 1953, just two years before Young's death. The razor blade was donated to the Museum in the late 1950s, along with a piece of wood that is believed to be the last piece ever chopped by Young, an active outdoorsman during and after his playing career.

The piece of wood, measuring $14\frac{1}{2}$ inches long and taken from a pile chopped by Young in 1954 at the home of William Shelton in Akron, Ohio, is signed by Young and dated November 8, 1954, just shy of a year before his death. The wood offers a substitute for a more traditional artifact, and it captures the essence of a player beyond his on-field feats. Seeing a glove used by Young can invoke memories of his dominance—a record 511 wins, which may never be matched—while a piece of chopped wood can remind every

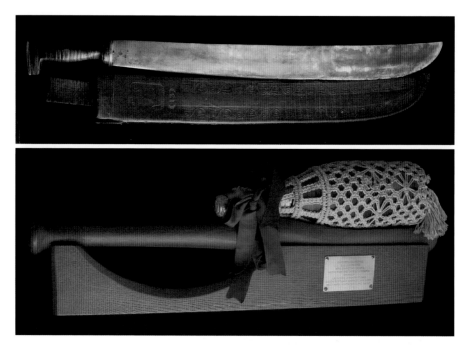

TOP: A machete used by American League founder Ban Johnson. ABOVE: The champagne bottle used to christen the naval freighter *Lou Gehrig*. OPPOSITE: An original light panel used to illuminate the scoreboard at Houston's Astrodome.

visitor that Young had hobbies beyond the ballparks in which he pitched.

The most recent offbeat addition to the Hall of Fame is the blood-stained sock worn by Boston Red Sox hurler Curt Schilling during Game Two of the 2004 World Series. The pitcher's ankle had been sutured to repair a torn muscle sheath, but the sutures bled during the game. As part of the Hall of Fame's collections from the Series, Schilling donated his spikes worn during the Series. After the hurler determined that the sock's rightful home was in the Red Sox display in Cooperstown, four months after the Series, Schilling's in-laws delivered the sock to the Museum to accompany his spikes.

A machete used by Ban Johnson, founder of the American League and a 1937 Hall of Fame inductee as an executive, offers a glimpse into the life of baseball's most influential executive for a quarter of a century. Johnson used the machete on hunting trips with fellow American League pioneer Charles Comiskey. The item was one of several Johnson items donated by Dr. George Massey of Lafayette, Indiana, in 1970.

Perhaps no player in baseball history has ever been as revered—then or now—as Lou Gehrig. Felled by a disease that would later take his name, Gehrig walked away from baseball in 1939 after he could no longer physically play the game, just before his thirty-sixth birthday. In January 1943, just eighteen months after his death, a Liberty Class 441 naval freighter named the *Lou Gehrig* was commissioned. The champagne bottle used to christen the ship by Gehrig's mother, Christine Gehrig, is a part of the Museum's collections.

In the 1960s, Sandy Koufax used a rubber inner tube to ice down his arm following his starts. This unorthodox method of rehabilitation was a harbinger of medical treatment to come in baseball, and though it was unique in form, it defined the rise of scientific contributions to the game.

Most fans count a baseball memory (or several hundred) from ballparks, either from their youth or in celebrating an indelible moment with the home team. A pinwheel from the original Comiskey Park scoreboard (pictured on page 39) highlights the Hall of Fame's exhibit Sacred Ground, which explores ballparks and the fan experience. Also on display in that exhibit is a five-bulb, two-circuit chip panel from the original Houston Astros scoreboard at the Astrodome. When the scoreboard was removed in 1988 to make room for more football seating, the Astros sent a panel of lights to Cooperstown to document the decades of memories for millions of Texans who recall the dazzling display of lights.

Though product endorsements and player advertising have been a part of baseball for more than 100 years, the rise of baseball superstars to national icons has been represented in many ways but perhaps most notably through the candy bar. The Cal Bar, Malley's Chipper Bar, and the David Justice Bar are just three chocolate confections that reside in the curatorial confines of Cooperstown, named for stars Cal Ripken Jr., Chipper Jones, and David Justice. Others to have graced the candy wrapper include Cecil Fielder, Ken Griffey Jr., and Hall of Famer Reggie Jackson.

From the interesting (a bowling pin presented to Rogers Hornsby) to the bizarre (an official Pittsburgh Green Weenie, distributed during the 1971 World Series by Pittsburgh radio station KDKA) to the insightful (a red Shriner's fez belonging to Ty Cobb, who belonged to the fraternal organization), artifacts can provide perspective in baseball history. A patch from the 1969 Seattle Pilots reminds viewers that the club had just a one-year existence in Seattle before moving to Milwaukee to become the Brewers.

Some artifact stories, like the petrified mitt that arrived in 1960, are not as complete and are best left to historical interpretation.

Education and Outreach
Beyond Cooperstown

To most people, the stately three-story redbrick building at 25 Main Street in Cooperstown is simply one of the world's best-known sports shrines. To teachers, students, and daily visitors, the National Baseball Hall of Fame and Museum is quickly becoming one of America's most respected cultural and educational destinations.

More than a showcase of bats, balls, and uniforms, the Baseball Hall of Fame is a treasure trove of cultural artifacts, documents, and legends that enlivens learning for fans of all ages. In fact, education is central to the Hall of Fame's mission. That emphasis, though, transcends the typical textbook approach.

The cornerstone of the Hall of Fame's education program, America Grows Inning by Inning, was developed by a committee of educators from Cooperstown and the surrounding area in 1991. The successful curriculum emphasizes an interactive, hands-on experience for students in grades four through eight. Critical thinking skills create the focus and provide a greater understanding of America's social history as reflected in the game of baseball. Using thirteen distinct learning modules, a direct correlation is made between classroom learning objectives and the surrounding world, as symbolized by the evolution of baseball as America's national pastime. After fourteen years, the program continues to experience steady growth—rising from 1,000 student visitors its first year to more than 7,000 students in the most recent school term.

Utilizing the same subjects covered in the on-site program, the Hall of Fame now reaches out to those students for whom Cooperstown is beyond a reasonable bus ride. The EBBETS Field Trip Series (Electronically Bringing Baseball Education To Students) offers live videoconferences featuring timeworn relics and primary source materials. Nearly 10,000 school-age children visit Cooperstown electronically each year, thanks in part to funding from the Institute for Museum and Library Services, as well as

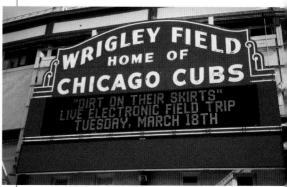

the Fund for the Improvement of Education. In 2005, an estimated 500 classrooms in thirty states, including Alaska and Hawaii, learned about history and a host of other subjects from the Museum's experienced educators.

Electronic Field Trips

For the past four years, the Hall of Fame has participated in five live and tape-delayed broadcasts to a nationwide audience of

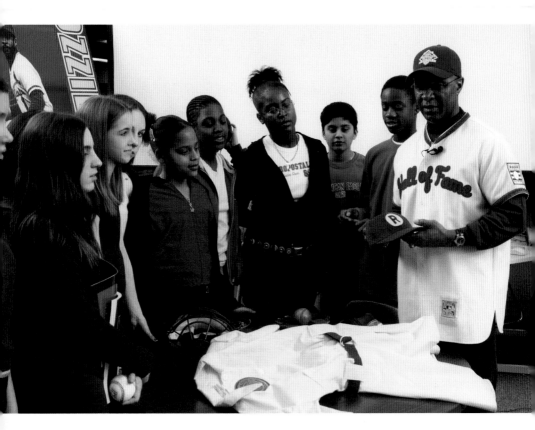

Hall of Fame education ambassador Ozzie Smith teaches a group of St. Louis area students about the history of uniforms and the role of women in baseball.

more than 100 million viewers. In conjunction with Ball State University in Muncie, Indiana, the Education Department has participated in electronic field trips that are televised to classrooms across the country through local PBS and cable affiliates.

Frank and Peggy Steele Internship Program

The latest piece of the outreach puzzle was the development and implementation of a first-rate internship program. The Frank and Peggy Steele Internship Program for Youth Leadership Development was established and endowed by Peggy Steele and is a fitting tribute to Peggy and her late husband Frank's longtime association with the Hall of Fame and their passion for youth education.

Admission into the program is highly competitive, as the Museum accepts twenty-five to thirty college-age students annually, granting participants a professional development experience and the opportunity of a lifetime. As part of the curriculum, the Museum offers trips to major league ballgames, career seminars, courses in professional development through brown-bag lunches with staff, and the chance to participate in the Museum's signature event of the year, Hall of Fame Weekend. The program is truly unique, and those who have participated have gone on to careers in baseball as well as in many other professional fields.

Baseball As America
Treasures Travel from Cooperstown

In 2002, Baseball As America, a national exhibition tour featuring 500 artifacts from the Museum's collection, opened a four-year tour to critical acclaim at the American Museum of Natural History in New York City. With ten scheduled stops through 2006, nearly 2.5 million visitors will have experienced Baseball As America. The national tour is sponsored by Ernst & Young.

Organized by the Hall of Fame and drawn from its unparalleled collections, this exhibition marks the first time that these Hall of Fame treasures have left their legendary home in Cooperstown. Through the exploration of a broad range of themes, including immigration, nationalism, integration, technology, and popular culture, Baseball As America reveals how baseball has both reflected and shaped American society.

Baseball As America will be on display in 2006 at the Henry Ford Museum in the Detroit,

Michigan, suburb of Dearborn through September 5. The tour has also visited New York City, Los Angeles, Chicago, Cincinnati, St. Petersburg (Florida), St. Louis, Houston, and Oakland. Four additional cities will be added to the Baseball As America tour through 2008.

For more information, and additional tour venues, please visit www.baseballasamerica.org.

Uniform worn by Jackie Robinson with the Brooklyn Dodgers, on tour with Baseball As America.

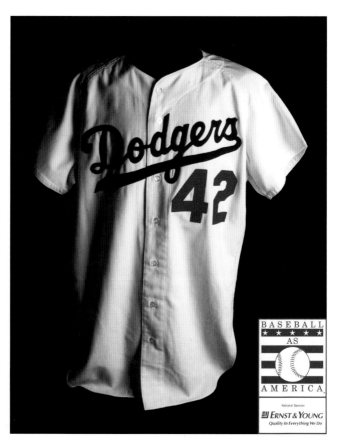

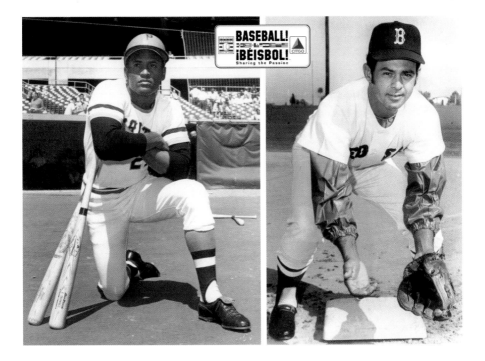

Baseball! ¡Béisbol!

The National Baseball Hall of Fame and Museum and CITGO Petroleum Corporation will launch a visitor experience tour in 2006 to bring the stories of Latino baseball to fans across the country. The project, entitled Baseball! ¡Béisbol!, will deliver two exhibitions to selected cities, featuring artifacts, imagery, and stories of Latin American baseball history and the contributions of Latino major league players and Hall of Fame members to our national pastime.

The first tour is scheduled to launch in late spring 2006 and features a two-dimensional exhibition in ten cities, exploring the contribution of each Caribbean nation and Mexico, while spotlighting the contributions of Latino major league players and Hall of Fame members. In 2008, a robust exhibition with artifacts and detailed histories will begin visiting major cities in the United States to relate the impact of Latin American countries on baseball today.

The partnership will continue through 2010 and will also result in a joint curatorial exchange between the National Baseball Hall of Fame and Museum and its Venezuelan and Caribbean counterparts; the translation to Spanish of all of the Hall of Fame plaques at the Museum's Web site and other printed materials; and other initiatives to detail baseball's rich history with Latin America.

Latino stars Roberto Clemente (LEFT) and Luis Aparicio are two Hall of Famers who will be featured in Baseball! ¡Béisbol!, a traveling exhibition from the Hall of Fame.

Around Cooperstown

Cooperstown is more than just baseball. Its Main Street way of life is supported by two additional world-class museums, a nationally renowned summer opera, a beautiful 9-mile-long lake, and deep historical roots that served as the basis for the novels of James Fenimore Cooper and his Leatherstocking Tales.

With a year-round population of just over 2,000 residents, the village of Cooperstown offers the simplicities of an earlier era. No large shopping malls can be found in the area, and the warm sense of community, bordered by the wooded hills and Otsego Lake, keep the region one of America's most treasured jewels.

Other attractions dot the landscape, providing the ultimate vacation destination for a wide range of travelers. Whether you are looking for a weekend getaway or a summer in paradise, be sure you visit these other village attractions.

The Otesaga Resort Hotel One of New York State's most distinctive

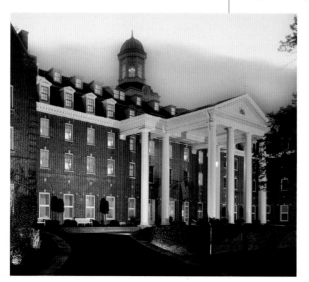

resorts, The Otesaga (BELOW) has operated since 1909 and is a member of the prestigious Historic Hotels of America. It is noted for its distinguished service, fine dining, renowned championship Leatherstocking Golf Course, and beautiful views. Visit www.otesaga.com.

Fenimore Art Museum This elegant 1930s neo-Georgian mansion features a showcase of premier collections of American art, including the acclaimed Eugene and Clare Thaw Collection of North American Indian Art. Visit www.fenimoreartmuseum.org.

The Farmers' Museum Step back in time and experience New York State history, where skilled artisans practice the trades and crafts of the nineteenth century. See authentically restored historic buildings and period furnishings, heritage gardens, rare breeds of farm animals, and more. Visit www.farmersmuseum.org.

Doubleday Field Operated by the village of Cooperstown, Doubleday Field hosts the annual Hall of Fame Game, featuring two major league teams, as well as more than 300 baseball games annually at every level of competition.

For more information on the village of Cooperstown and the year-round schedule of events and activities, please contact the Cooperstown Chamber of Commerce by phone at (607) 547-9931 or via the Web at www.cooperstownchamber.org.

How to Support
the Hall of Fame

Preserving History. Honoring Excellence. Connecting Generations.

The Mission of the National Baseball Hall of Fame and Museum

The National Baseball Hall of Fame and Museum is an educational institution dedicated to fostering an appreciation of the historical development of baseball and its impact on our culture, through collecting, preserving, exhibiting, and interpreting its collections for a global audience, as well as honoring those who have made outstanding contributions to the sport.

Supporting the Hall of Fame

As a nonprofit organization, independent of Major League Baseball, the Hall of Fame depends on support from a variety of sources and at many different levels to maintain its operations. Since opening its doors for the first time in 1939, each artifact in the Hall of Fame's possession has been donated.

The Hall of Fame welcomes monetary gifts ranging from annual fund gifts, matching funds, endowment giving, bequests, and more. For information on how you can support the Hall of Fame, please contact the Hall of Fame Development Office at (607) 547-0333.

Friends of the Hall of Fame Program

The most convenient way to support the National Baseball Hall of Fame and Museum is to become a Friends of the Hall of Fame member. Friends members receive benefits at a variety of levels, while helping to support the Hall of Fame's mission and educational programs. Individual memberships start at $40.

Benefits to the Friends of the Hall of Fame program include a subscription to the bimonthly magazine *Memories and Dreams*, the official publication of the National Baseball Hall of Fame and Museum; the annual Hall of Fame Yearbook, featuring bios of Hall of Fame members; free shipping and 10 percent off retail purchases made on-site and online; and free admission to the Museum throughout the year.

For higher levels of Friends membership, opportunities are available, including reserved Induction Ceremony seating; special event access with Hall of Fame members; and limited edition gifts, such as lithographs and paintings.

You can learn more about becoming a Friend of the Hall of Fame today by visiting the Membership Desk in the Museum lobby, enrolling online at www.baseballhalloffame.org, or calling (607) 547-0397.

OPPOSITE: The Otesaga Resort Hotel in Cooperstown.

Hall of Fame Events

Baseball's Legends Return Each July

The signature special event of the National Baseball Hall of Fame and Museum, Hall of Fame Weekend offers visitors to Cooperstown an opportunity to see the largest congregation of living legends, while honoring the newest electees to the sport's greatest shrine. Held the final weekend in July every year, Hall of Fame Weekend provides entertainment for fans of all eras, highlighted by the Induction Ceremony on Sunday, in which fifty to sixty Hall of Famers return to welcome the newest inductees. Additionally, awards are presented to a baseball broadcaster for excellence and to a baseball writer for meritorious contributions to the game.

Hall of Fame Weekend features events such as Connecting Generations, in which Hall of Fame members participate in a trivia contest, a Legends Series event in which the newest inductees discuss their careers, book signings in the Museum, special edition Sandlot Stories presentations, and much more. Your baseball card collection comes to life in Cooperstown the final weekend of July, as baseball's brightest luminaries return to the pastoral setting to honor the game's elite.

Hall of Fame Game

Every year since 1940, two major league teams have been scheduled to play an exhibition game in Cooperstown, the annual Hall of Fame Game. The only in-season exhibition game permitted by Major League Baseball, the Hall of Fame Game traditionally pits an American League team against a National League team at historic Doubleday Field, a 10,000-seat stadium located on Main Street, just blocks from the Hall of Fame.

Since the Hall of Fame Game was separated from Hall of Fame Weekend in 2003, a full weekend of programming and special guests augments the traditional Monday classic.

Programming Activities and Special Events

In addition to Hall of Fame Weekend and the Hall of Fame Game, the Museum offers more than 1,000 programming events over the course of the year, ranging from the All-Star Game and World Series galas to rookie workshops designed for the young visitor. Daily programming runs throughout the summer months, with special events, anniversary celebrations, and activities for visitors of all ages scheduled year-round.

Boston's Johnny Damon signs autographs for fans during the 2005 Hall of Fame Game at Doubleday Field.

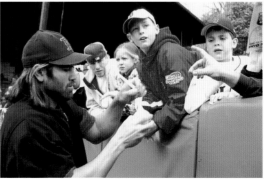

Take Cooperstown Home with You

Museum Store

The Museum Store resides on the first floor and provides a fitting ending to your Hall of Fame journey. Visit the Store for unique gifts, keepsakes, and clothing apparel for yourself and the baseball fans in your life. Your purchases help to support the Hall of Fame and its not-for-profit educational mission.

While visiting the Museum Store, sign up to receive a merchandise catalog; *Inside Pitch*, the Hall of Fame's free weekly e-mail newsletter; a trial copy of *Memories and Dreams*, the Hall of Fame's official magazine; and send a digital postcard to friends around the world from the National Baseball Hall of Fame and Museum.

Museum Bookstore

Also be sure to visit the Museum Bookstore, located in the Library Atrium, which carries a wide variety of books and videos on many baseball subjects. Popular book signings take place in the adjacent Library Atrium year-round, and signed books and many others can be purchased from the Bookstore.

Photo Collection

The National Baseball Hall of Fame Library contains nearly 500,000 original photographs detailing the game's illustrious history, from the 1840s to today.

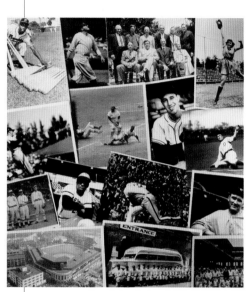

Featuring Hall of Famers, teams, stadiums, historic events, players, Negro league stars, the AAGPBL, and others, the collection's rich selection of photos appeals to every fan of each era of our national game. Each photo offered is a reprint of the original image in the permanent collection of the Hall of Fame Library.

Order images in the Museum Store, online at www.baseballhalloffame.org, or by calling (607) 547-0372.

Visit Our Web Site Year-Round

Once your journey through Cooperstown is complete, stay in touch through the Hall's Web site, www.baseballhalloffame.org. With more than 2,000 pages of content, you can research Hall of Fame players, read original content, participate in live streaming events, and much more.

Photographs from the Hall of Fame's photo collection are available at the Museum Store.

Photo Credits

Plaque commemorating the first induction in 1939.

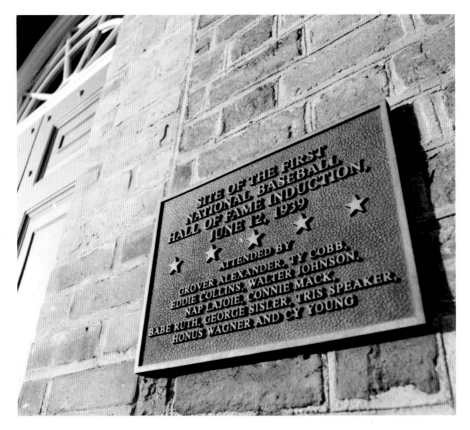